AF126337

BOOK ANALYSIS

Written by Élodie Veysseyre
Translated by Rebecca Neal

Thirteen Reasons Why
by Jay Asher

JAY ASHER

AMERICAN NOVELIST

- **Born in Arcadia, California in 1975.**
- **Notable works:**
  - *The Future of Us* (2011), novel, co-written with Carolyn Mackler
  - *What Light* (2016), novel
  - *Piper* (2017), graphic novel, co-written with Jessica Freeburg and illustrated by Jeff Stokely

Jay Asher is an American novelist; his first novel, *Thirteen Reasons Why*, was published in 2007.

He generally writes for a young adult readership and explores the upheaval and difficulties faced by American teenagers, dealing with themes including bullying at school, suicide, violence, guilt and betrayal. The setting of his fiction is always realistic: his novels are all set in modern-day American high schools, and sometimes feature social media.

Asher is one of the USA's most popular young adult fiction writers, and Thirteen Reasons Why has topped the prestigious New York Times Best Seller List.

THIRTEEN REASONS WHY

A SHOCKING STORY OF HARASSMENT AND BULLYING AT SCHOOL

- **Genre:** young adult novel
- **Reference edition:** Asher, J. (2011) *Thirteen Reasons Why*. New York: Razorbill.
- **1ˢᵗ edition:** 2007
- **Themes:** bullying, suicide, guilt, American school system, violence, friendship, betrayal

13 Reasons Why is an American novel which was published in 2007. It is set in the present day in an American high school which has been left reeling by the suicide of one of its pupils, Hannah Baker. Before her suicide, she recorded 13 cassette tapes outlining the reasons behind her decision. Her friend Clay Jensen sets out to investigate, although to begin with he is completely unaware of the terrible ordeals she had endured. Listening to the tapes profoundly and permanently alters his outlook on life.

SUMMARY

After Hannah Baker commits suicide, one of her classmates, Clay Jensen, receives a strange package containing seven audio tapes. He realises that the tapes were recorded by Hannah before her death to explain the 13 reasons for her suicide. Clay begins to investigate and gradually gathers Hannah's many secrets to piece together the puzzle of her death.

HANNAH BAKER'S SECRET TAPES

Clay Jensen discovers a package containing seven audio tapes on his doorstep. His curiosity is awakened and he borrows an old cassette player from his classmate Tony to listen to them. He is stunned to realise that they were recorded by Hannah Baker, a girl from his high school who committed suicide a few weeks ago.

On each side of the tapes (13 in total), Hannah recounts a significant event from towards the end of her life, in which one person in particular played an important role. Each of these people nudged her a little closer to suicide through their behaviour, their conscious or unconscious malice or their insensitivity.

Clay is shocked, especially when he realises that one of the tapes is addressed to him. However, he does not know why and is assailed by doubt, worrying that he too helped drive Hannah to suicide.

As he listens to the tapes, he discovers a series of shocking secrets as Hannah unflinchingly describes her experiences in the last months of her life. These range from being betrayed by friends she had trusted to intrusions into her private life to sexual assault and even rape. To make his "investigation" feel more real and to give himself some idea of the ordeals his classmate endured, each time Clay listens to a tape he visits the place where the events it describes took place, including Hannah's favourite shop, the café where she used to meet up with her friends and the cinema where she worked with him.

In addition to listening to the tapes and visiting these locations, Clay meets people and tells them about what he is learning. At the café, he meets Skye, a brooding, strange, antisocial former acquaintance who he lost touch with years ago. When he is listening to the side of the tape addressed to him, he runs into Tony, who seems to know a lot more about the tapes than he is letting on...

A CONVERSATION FROM BEYOND THE GRAVE

The tape reveals that Hannah and Clay kissed during a party with their classmates. That evening, Hannah, who was overwhelmed by dark memories and traumatised by recent events, told Clay to leave her alone. He did so, oblivious to the true extent of her suffering.

While he is listening to the tape, Clay is drawn into an improbable conversation with Hannah in which he tries to justify himself and gives his version of events. Unlike the rest of the people on the tapes, he is not truly guilty of anything, but he still feels very guilty.

When Clay has finished listening, Tony tells him that he was the last person to see Hannah and that he helped her to get hold of the cassettes, although he did not know what she was planning to do with them.

A DESCENT INTO HELL

As Clay listens to the remaining tapes, he is stunned by the secrets he uncovers and finally begins to grasp just how much pain Hannah was in.

Doubt, fear and guilt then give way to anger and a sense of powerlessness. He realises that a lot of Hannah's ordeals could have been prevented, but it is too late now: the tapes have been recorded and the damage is done.

In Cassette 5: Side A and Cassette 6: Side B, Clay learns that Hannah was first a witness to and then a victim of rape. Both rapes were committed by a classmate, Bryce Walker. Clay feels powerless, as all he can do at this stage is listen to Hannah's tapes. It is a traumatic experience for him, as he finally becomes fully conscious of the hell Hannah was going through but knows that it is too late to do anything about it. Clay repeatedly utters the word "God" as he listens to the tapes in an involuntary expression of his unease and sense of powerlessness.

The final tape is also one of the most important. It recounts a conversation between Hannah and Mr. Porter, the school guidance counsellor. He is the only adult mentioned in the tapes. In this conversation, Hannah told Mr. Porter that she was struggling and wanted to end it all so that she could finally be free, but Clay is stunned to discover that the counsellor apparently failed to grasp the gravity of the situation. Hannah ended up leaving his office without receiving an answer or any help.

A NEW BEGINNING FOR CLAY?

After he has finished listening to the tapes, Clay realises that Hannah's suicide could have been avoided if only people had seen the signs. He meets Skye again, and this new encounter is decisive. Clay wonders whether she is also suffering in silence, unnoticed by everyone else, and whether this time he could act and prevent another tragedy.

CHARACTER STUDY

CLAY JENSEN

Clay Jensen is the novel's narrator and main character. He is a student at an American high school, and discovers a box of audio cassettes addressed to him. He realises that these tapes were recorded by his classmate Hannah Baker, who died a few weeks previously, and that they contain weighty secrets, as she has used them to explain all the reasons for her suicide.

Clay is an ordinary, somewhat reserved student. As he listens to the tapes, he realises that nobody had understood how much Hannah was suffering or the ordeals that she had endured. Even though Clay worked with her, went to school with her and had gone to a party with her, he too remained oblivious.

Clay quickly becomes obsessed with the tapes and is completely drawn in by Hannah's story. He is determined "to understand. Whatever it takes" (p. 101), although he initially refuses to follow the instructions she gives in the tapes. In the end, he follows her instructions to the letter and visits every place Hannah mentions in a bid to understand her better.

Clay changes a great deal over the course of the novel. At the start of the story, he is convinced that he bears no responsibility for his friend's death. However, as the tapes progress, doubts begin to creep in and he soon starts to feel guilty, as he wonders whether the fact that he did nothing to stop what was happening means that he was also partly responsible. As the events Hannah described become more violent and traumatic, he experiences a growing sense of unease and powerlessness. By the end of the novel, his sense of guilt and his grief for Hannah have abated somewhat, and he wants to take action to help another of his classmates, who he fears could end up like his friend.

As such, both Clay and the reader learn a lot in the course of the novel. As the story is written in the first person, the reader feels directly involved. We find out key pieces of information at the same time as Clay and follow his investigation at the same pace. We also end up sharing some of his feelings: guilt and powerlessness, but also hope and relief as the novel progresses.

HANNAH BAKER

Hannah committed suicide several weeks before Clay discovers the audio cassettes. This means that she is physically absent from the narrative and never interacts directly with the other characters. However, her presence can be felt throughout the story: she talks through the tapes and Clay remembers some of the experiences they shared.

She is a tragic character who wanted to explain the reasons for her suicide in order to help her loved ones understand and possibly to spare others from the same fate. In her explanation, she publicly accuses a number of her classmates and neighbours, as well as her school guidance counsellor, of being partly responsible for her suicide. In this sense, the tapes also serve as a kind of posthumous vengeance.

From a psychological point of view, Hannah is far from fragile; on the contrary, she is a strong, determined character who overcame a number of ordeals and setbacks before eventually being overwhelmed. This inner strength drives her to record the tapes to expose what happened to her and to punish those responsible. However, we get the impression that her will to live is ebbing as she endures a series of increasingly tragic events: by the end of the recording, Hannah is more determined than ever, but channels this determination into going through with her suicide rather than continuing to live.

Hannah is an unusual character for a young adult novel. Although she could be described as the story's protagonist, and even as its heroine, she is physically absent from it. However, the fact that her recorded voice is omnipresent throughout means that it is easy for the reader to forget that she is not physically present. She even manages to have a sort of conversation with Clay through the tapes, and their exchanges are very realistic.

THE SUBJECTS OF THE TAPES

Hannah's audio tapes target 12 people (not 13, as the novel's title suggests, because Cassette 5: Side B is addressed to two individuals who are dealt with in other sides, namely Justin and

Bryce). Clay does not meet with most of the characters from the tapes in the course of the novel; this means that they are absent from the story and Hannah's descriptions of their behaviour are the only information we are given about them. The characters on the tapes are:

- **Justin Foley** (Cassette 1: Side A and Cassette 5: Side B), Hannah's first boyfriend. He spreads a "rumor based on a kiss [which] started a reputation that other people believed in and reacted to" (p. 30). This broke Hannah's heart, as she thought that he was honest and sincere in his love for her.

- **Alex Standall** (Cassette 1: Side B), an acquaintance of Hannah's who made her life difficult when he voted her "Best Ass in the Freshman Class" (p. 37). In doing so, he involuntarily further tarnished her reputation, which had already been damaged by her relationship with Justin.

- **Jessica Davis** (Cassette 2: Side A), a former friend of Hannah's. The two girls fell out when Jessica preferred to believe the rumours circulating about Hannah at school rather than taking her friend at her word.

- **Tyler Down** (Cassette 2: Side B), a fellow student, amateur photographer and voyeur who spied on Hannah at home.
- **Courtney Crimsen** (Cassette 3: Side A), one of Hannah's acquaintances who used her to stay popular.
- **Marcus Cole** (Cassette 3: Side B), who tried to sexually assault her.
- **Zachary Dempsey** (Cassette 4: Side A), a friend of Marcus's who was rejected by Hannah and decided to take revenge by stealing messages addressed to her.
- **Ryan Shaver** (Cassette 4: Side B), who stole a poem that Hannah had written and published it against her will.
- **Jenny Kurtz** (Cassette 6: Side A), an acquaintance of Hannah's. She caused a fatal accident which Hannah witnessed, but never admitted responsibility for it and continued to act as though nothing had happened.
- **Bryce Walker** (Cassette 5: Side B and Cassette 6: Side A), an acquaintance of Hannah's who is abusive and violent. He raped one of Hannah's classmates, and later Hannah herself.
- **Mr. Porter** (Cassette 7: Side A), the school guidance counsellor. When Hannah told him

that she wanted to commit suicide, he made no attempt to stop her.

THE GUARDIAN ANGELS

There are two characters who play a significant role in the novel but could not be described as protagonists:

- **Tony Padilla**, a fellow student. Hannah entrusted him with the tapes, but as soon as he realised what she was planning to do, he tried to stop her. However, his efforts were in vain. He acts as Clay's guardian angel when Clay discovers what is on the tapes.
- **Lainie Jensen**, Clay's mother, who appears frequently in the story to check on Clay. She repeatedly tries to help him while he is listening to the tapes, but each time he rebuffs her.

ANALYSIS

THE SEARCH FOR THE TRUTH

The structure of the story is based on Clay's mental and physical journey towards the truth behind his friend's death.

Clay does not simply listen to the tapes Hannah recorded: he physically follows in her footsteps as she describes the defining events of the end of her life. Each side of the tapes is focused on a character, a particular event and the place where this event occurred. Clay does everything he can to get closer to Hannah and travels to all the places she describes in an attempt to relive her experiences.

This movement between several key locations plays a significant role in the narrative. As well as giving Clay a better understanding of the events he is listening to and leading him along a tangible path towards the truth, it also creates a link between the moment in the past as Hannah experienced it and the moment in the present as Clay is experiencing it.

The places described by Hannah in the tapes come to life when she meets people and undergoes decisive experiences. By the time Clay visits them, at dusk and then in the middle of the night, they are "dead": they are plunged into darkness, deserted or closed. This serves to accentuate the story's dramatic, tragic dimension. Moreover, the fact that they are shrouded in darkness and silence reminds us that it is too late, that what is done is done and that Hannah is dead.

Throughout the story, a number of parallels are drawn between Hannah's narrative and Clay's journey:

- Clay visits the places Hannah described to relive her experience her experiences in real time.
- Whether voluntarily or involuntarily, Clay replicates the same actions in the same places: for example, he buys the same items that Hannah bought in the same shop and drinks a milkshake in the spot she recommends in the restaurant. In this way, the reader too seems to relive Hannah's experiences.
- Sometimes there is a kind of dialogue between Clay and Hannah's recording. Throughout

the novel, the text of the recording is written in italics to differentiate it from Clay's voice. Clay's narrative is written in the first person and is interspersed with extracts from the tapes and Hannah's constant questions and interjections. This generates a sense of unease and gives the impression that the voice on the cassette is in some way intruding into the narrative. Clay rarely pauses the recordings, but he regularly adds his own comments on them.

• These exchanges culminate when Clay listens to the tape addressed to him, in which Hannah speaks directly to him through the recording and Clay constantly responds, as though she were sitting opposite him. The resulting dialogue seems like a natural conversation, and the reader almost forgets that the two characters are not speaking at the same time and that one of them is dead.

These parallels temporarily bring Hannah back to life. Even though she is dead, Clay is able to talk to her, share experiences with her and come to understand her better. The novel is rich in vocabulary relating to the senses, particularly the sense of hearing: throughout the story, Clay also experiences the sounds in the recording, such as a "rustling of leaves" (p. 90), a "slow breath of air" (p. 282) and the sound of Hannah "uncrinkling a piece of paper" (p. 41). When he listens to the cassette, he feels as though she is in front of him and "stand[s] and watch[es] her image disappear" (p. 45).

The passage of time is also significant in the novel. The time of the narration is clearly defined: it begins when Clay receives the tapes one evening and ends the next morning, after he has listened to them all. This means that the narrative spans a very short period of time, which is unusual for a young adult novel. This is a deliberate choice on the part of the author:

- It demonstrates how the narrator becomes obsessed with the tapes and rushes to get to the end of them. Like the reader, he is eager to find out what happened and forgets about his own daily life to do so. The fact that he listens to the tapes one after the other and seems to lose touch with reality while he is listening to them adds to the impression of obsession and a compulsive "need to understand. Whatever it takes" (p. 101).

- The story takes place entirely at night, which adds a symbolic dimension. Clay starts listening to the tapes at dusk, but as the night progresses, the growing darkness mirrors the increasingly violent and traumatic events recounted by Hannah. By dawn, Clay has become a new person, with a wisdom that he did not possess the day before. He is ready to face the challenges of his new life as a young adult and put the experience he has acquired overnight into practice.

GENRE: TRAGEDY, EPISTOLARY NOVEL, YOUNG ADULT FICTION AND COMING-OF-AGE STORY

Thirteen Reasons Why is a young adult novel, but the influence of several other genres is clearly visible throughout the book.

Tragedy

The novel features a number of the key characteristics of tragedy:

- We know from the start that the story will have an unhappy ending. The reader's aim is therefore not to find out whether Hannah Baker will die, but rather how and why she will die.

- Throughout the novel, the reader feels powerless in the face of a series of increasingly tragic events, which seem to be inevitable.
- The reader, along with some of the characters, such as Clay and Tony, experiences catharsis. A terrible event has occurred, and the reader and these characters are trying to understand the reasons for it in order to exorcise their pain and grief.

Catharsis

Catharsis (from the Greek for "purification") was theorised by Aristotle (Greek philosopher, 384-322 BCE) in his *Poetics* (c. 335 BCE). According to this concept, when the spectator is faced with traumatic events (most often in a tragic play) which inspire pity or fear in them, they are purified of their passions and released from their emotions.

Epistolary novel

The novel also has some of the features of the epistolary genre, which refers to stories that are written in the form of a series of letters. Hannah speaks through cassette tapes recorded before her death, which means that she is communicating indirectly with her listeners, who are listening at a different time and in a different place. This creates an unbridgeable distance: by the time the recordings are discovered, it is too late to save her, which increases the listener's (and the reader's) sense of powerlessness.

It is interesting that Hannah chose to record her last thoughts on audio cassettes, as the novel was published in 2007 and this medium was already declining in the 1990s. Indeed, audio cassettes are very rarely used nowadays, as Clay notes (p. 6); he also struggles to get hold of a cassette player to listen to them.

Written messages such as letters would not have had the same effect on the reader. The use of tapes adds to the drama of the story:

- Tapes are "dead" objects for the novel's characters and readers, which establishes an obvious link between the medium and the sender of the message.
- Unlike letters, phone calls and so on, cassette

tapes do not invite a response. The sender's tragic fate is irrevocable.
- The tapes are a way of hearing the dead person's voice for the last time, and therefore of bringing them back to life in a way.
- Beyond their symbolism, cassette tapes are intriguing for young people as they are rare and unfamiliar.

Young adult fiction

Although the epistolary form is undeniably unusual for young adult fiction, the novel is still clearly part of the genre and exhibits many of its typical features: it is set in a school, many of the events and interactions it depicts are linked to this setting, and it portrays relationships between teenagers, which are often instinctual and violent.

The story's setting is very realistic. The novel depicts the day-to-day lives of American high school students; although their experience will not necessary be identical to that of readers from other countries, it will be largely familiar.

The novel's realism accentuates its uncomfortable, frightening aspect, as the violent, shocking events depicted contrast with the familiar, "safe" setting.

Coming-of-age story

The novel could be described as a coming-of-age story. In the course of the narrative, Clay learns a lot not only about Hannah, but also about himself and his relationships with other people. At the start of the novel, he is detached and does not seem to care very much about the world around him, but by the end he is much more engaged and is eager to act to change things. For example, it is implied that he wants to help another classmate who is struggling. This dimension of the story is reinforced by the symbolism of his geographic and mental journey towards the truth as he spends a night listening to the tapes.

RECEPTION

When the novel was published, and particularly when it was adapted into a Netflix series, it sparked lively debate about suicide and school bullying. Its realism meant that some critics claimed that its treatment of suicide and exploration of the reasons young people commit suicide is too explicit. The series also caused controversy with its shocking, crudely depicted scenes of rape and suicide.

With this in mind, when studying the novel it is necessary to proceed with caution and keep in mind that, in spite of its realism, it is still a work of fiction.

The novel and its television adaptation can be seen as a manifesto against school bullying, which has various causes, can take numerous forms and may have devastating consequences. It uses the 13 sides of the tape to illustrate some of the reasons people commit suicide. However, the novel's message cannot be reduced to this list, and Asher (through the character of Hannah) stresses that the suicide it depicts is the result of a "snowball effect" (p. 273) as a series of traumatic events occur in quick succession.

SOME HELPFUL RESOURCES

The following resources may be useful for readers in the UK:

- Bullying at school

- ○ <u>Bullying UK</u>, which aims to offer support and advice to families affected by bullying.
- ○ <u>Understanding Bullying</u>, a resource produced for parents by the BBC.
- ○ The <u>Bullying at School</u> page of the gov.uk websites, which provides guidance on reporting bullying and on victims' legal rights.

- Suicide
  - ○ <u>Samaritans</u>, a suicide prevention organisation for all ages.
  - ○ <u>Papyrus</u>, which is dedicated to preventing suicide among young people.
  - ○ <u>Childline</u>, which allows under-19s to talk confidentially to a trained counsellor by phone, email or chat.
  - ○ The <u>NHS</u> website, which provides information on dealing with mental health crises and the numbers of suicide prevention helplines.

DID YOU KNOW?

Jay Asher and members of the cast and crew of the series have spoken out to clarify their message and encourage viewers to seek help if they are struggling. In particular, they have launched a <u>website</u> dedicated to suicide prevention and school bullying which aims to encourage those affected to talk to their loved ones or a dedicated mental health professional.

FURTHER REFLECTION

SOME QUESTIONS TO THINK ABOUT...

- Two literary works are mentioned in the course of the novel. What are they? In what ways can they be compared to Asher's novel?
- Research the rules and aims of classical tragedy. Which of these rules does the novel follow?
- Asher uses a large amount of sensory vocabulary to give the character of Hannah a more tangible presence in the text. Identify at least two examples for each of the five senses.
- Over what time period does the story unfold? Why? What effect does this have on the reader?
- What places does Clay visit while he is listening to the tapes? At what point does he visit each of them? What effect do these visits have on his experience of listening to the tapes?
- Who is the narrator of the story? What kind of narration is used, and what effect does it have on the reader?

- In your opinion, why did Asher choose to have Hannah tell her story through audio cassettes?
- Identify passages in which Hannah is compared to a supernatural presence, visible to Clay at certain points in the narrative. How is this character described?

We want to hear from you!
Leave a comment on your online library
and share your favourite books on social media!

FURTHER READING

REFERENCE EDITION

- Asher, J. (2011) *Thirteen Reasons Why*. New York: Razorbill.

REFERENCE STUDY

- Leloup, D. (2017) Sur Internet, la série « 13 Reasons Why » provoque un vaste débat à propos du suicide. *Le Monde*. [Online]. [Accessed 25 October 2018]. Available from: <https://www.lemonde.fr/pixels/article/2017/04/16/la-serie-13-reasons-why-provoque-une-discussion-geante-a-propos-du-suicide_5112021_4408996.html>

ADAPTATION

- *13 Reasons Why*. (2017-present) [Television series]. Created by Brian Yorkey. USA: July Moon Productions, Kicked to the Curb Productions, Anonymous Content, Paramount Television.

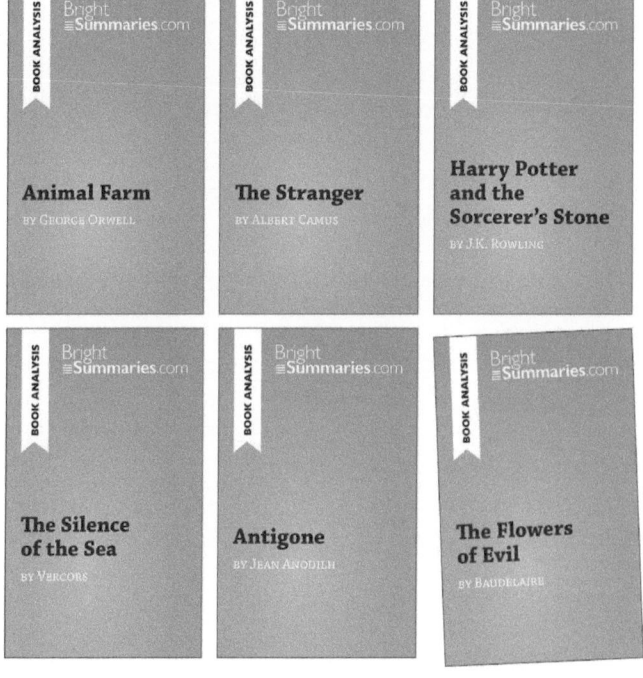

www.brightsummaries.com

Ebook EAN: 9782808013796

Paperback EAN: 9782808013802

Legal Deposit: D/2018/12603/449

Cover: © Primento

Digital conception by Primento, the digital partner of publishers.